SLAVERY

SLAVERY

The many faces of a Southern institution

Peter J. Parish

KEELEUNIVERSITY**PRESS**

First published in 1979
Reprinted 1979, 1982, 1984
1985, 1986, 1988, 1992, 1998, 2000, 2004
© British Association for American Studies, 1979

Transferred to digital print 2009

Typeset by Carnegie Publishing Ltd
18 Maynard Street, Preston

Printed and bound in Great Britain by
CPI Antony Rowe, Chippenham and Eastbourne

ISBN 1-85331-201-0

CONTENTS

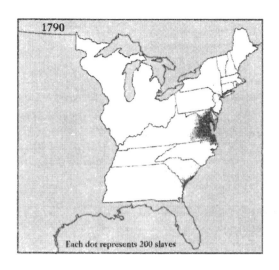

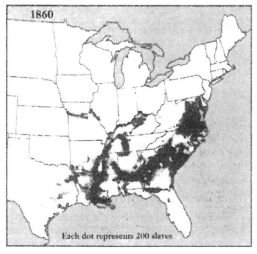

The distribution of the slave population
in 1790 and 1860

ACKNOWLEDGEMENTS

We are grateful to the Carnegie Institute of Washington for permission to reproduce the maps on p. vi, and to the John Judkyn Memorial for permission to reproduce the handbill illustrated on the cover. This handbill is advertising a slave auction in New Orleans in 1855. It is interesting to note the credit mechanisms involved, and the intention of selling slaves by "families". Louisiana was unusual in prohibiting the sale of slaves under the age of 10 apart from their mothers. The auctioneer belonged to a well-known and respected family in New Orleans.

The photograph on p. 35 is taken from Alan Thomas, *The Expanding Eye: Photography and the Nineteenth-Century Mind* (London: 1977); attempts to trace the owner of the copyright have failed.

Oxford University Press of New York kindly permitted us to quote from Lawrence W. Levine, *Black Culture and Black Consciousness: Afro-American Folk Thought from Slavery to Freedom* (1977).

1. The paradoxical institution

In the American South, as elsewhere, slavery rested upon a basic contradiction. Its guiding principle was that slaves were property, but its everyday practice demonstrated the impossibility of living up to, or down to, that denial of the slave's humanity. The master learned to treat his slaves both as property and as men; the slave learned how to express and affirm his humanity even while he was constrained in much of his life to accept his status as a chattel.

For all the harsh lines of status and class, race and colour, which divided owners and slaves, both were caught up in a complex web of compromise, adjustment, inconsistency, ambiguity and deception. Slave society was the society of the double standard, adopted for its own convenience by the' slaveowning class, and forced upon the slaves by the simple need to survive. For the master, there were the competing demands of profit and paternalism, economic interest and social status. The master claimed the absolute right of an owner over his property, but he was also restrained by the conventional morality of his time, his own standards of

1

decency and the pressure of the white community. Owners weighed both their interests and their principles when they debated the balance between kindness and severity, the carrot and the stick, persuasion and coercion, in their management of their slaves.

For their part, slaves were obliged to strike their own balance between resignation and rebellion, accommodation to the facts of slave life and resistance to the dominance of their masters. In their daily lives they strove to reconcile the demands of survival with the impulse to assert their autonomy. They struggled to create and maintain a life a situation where their lives were patently not entirely their own. They hated slavery but could not maintain total hatred of slaveowners and their families. They could fight or take flight or they could lapse into total submissiveness, but for most of the time most slaves steered a complex, devious, often inconsistent and confused course between those two extremes.

Lawrence Levine has highlighted some of the more acute paradoxes of slavery for both masters and slaves:

Slaveholders who considered Afro-Americans to be little more than sub-human chattels converted them to a religion which stressed their humanity and even their divinity. Masters who desired and expected their slaves to act like dependent children also enjoined them to behave like mature, responsible adults ... Whites who considered their black servants to be little more than barbarians, bereft of any culture worth the name, paid a fascinated and flattering attention to their song, their dance, their tales, and their form of religious exercise. The life of every slave could be altered by the most arbitrary and amoral acts. They could be whipped, sexually assaulted, ripped out of societies in which they had deep roots, and bartered away for pecuniary profit by men and women who were also capable of treating them with kindness and consideration and who professed belief in a moral code which they held up for emulation not only by their children but often by their slaves as well.[1]

In their different ways whites and blacks, masters and slaves, learned to live with slavery by learning to "live a lie". They divided their lives into compartments, did not prize consistency too highly, and blurred the harsh lines of the system by bargain and compromise.

These inner tensions reveal themselves in much of the historical debate about slavery. Traditionally the slave has been cast in the role of object, as either victim or beneficiary, and historians have argued about the relative harshness or mildness of the regime. The answers they have given have often related to their views of the slave economy, of the efficiency or inefficiency of slave labour. The first great historian of slavery, the Southerner Ulrich B. Phillips, treated the slave as beneficiary of a patriarchal but unprofitable institution designed to maintain the South's cardinal principle of white supremacy.[2] By contrast, the distinguished Northern historian Kenneth M. Stampp a generation later saw the slave as the maltreated victim of a profitable economic system.[3] Even Fogel and Engerman, in their recent, supposedly path-breaking "cliometric" work *Time on the Cross*, fall within this tradition. For they argue that the slave benefited in many ways, simply because considerate treatment of a valuable capital asset was to the financial advantage of profit-seeking slaveowners. Where Phillips viewed slavery as mild but inefficient and Stampp saw it as harsh but profitable, Fogel and Engerman describe an institution which was at once mild, efficient and profitable.[4]

The leading characteristic of recent work, however, has been the belated recognition of the slave as a person. In the last twenty years, historical dispute has become concerned also about the extent to which the slave personality resisted, or succumbed to, the extraordinary stresses of bondage, and the ways in which slaves succeeded in constructing and maintaining a life style, a set of values, a culture which was distinctively their own. In his *Slavery: a Problem in American Institutional and Intellectual Life*, Stanley Elkins saw the slave as the psychic casualty of an all-embracing repressive system. It is partly in reaction against Elkins and other interpretations of the slave as victim or object that a number of recent historians – Eugene Genovese, Herbert Gutman, Lawrence Levine, John Blassingame and others – have portrayed the slave as an active participant in the development of his own life style, and have sought to present a slave's eye view of slavery. However, if these historians have raised new questions and offered new perspectives, they show no sign of agreeing on new answers.[5]

The complexity of the problem derives from not only the contradictions but also the variety of slavery in the American South. There can be no greater mistake than to regard slavery as monolithic. It evolved over two centuries before it reached its prime in the pre-Civil War decades and some major recent interpretations have neglected this most important historical dimension. The institution of slavery varied greatly too from place to place, from the border states to the Deep South, from Virginia through the Carolinas to Mississippi and Texas. It differed also according to the demands made by various staple crops cotton, tobacco, sugar, rice. It varied most of all perhaps according to the size of the individual slaveholding unit. Historians have understandably given most of their attention to the larger plantations, and the stock image of the slave environment is the great plantation, with its scores or even hundreds of slaves. In fact, in the mid-nineteenth century half of the total number of slaveholders owned no more than five slaves each. Slavery was a system of many systems, with numerous exceptions to every rule. There were urban slaves, industrial slaves, and hired slaves, and there were a quarter of a million free blacks in the South who lived constantly in the shadow of slavery. Slaves were domestic servants, craftsmen and artisans, overseers and drivers, as well as field hands.

Finally the variety of slavery arose from the variety of human nature. Slaveowners and slaves, like other men, could be honest or dishonest, weak or strong, responsible or irresponsible, humane or sadistic, puritanical or lecherous, sober or drunk, stable or neurotic, intelligent or stupid. If the impact of slavery upon the slave depended upon the character, and the mood, of the master, the response of the slave to his situation depended upon his individual resources of character, will, endurance and adaptability, and the sustaining power of his family, his community, his faith and his way of life. Behind all the generalizations, the models and the stereotypes about the planter class, the slave personality and the slave community, there lies the history of million of individuals living out their daily lives.

2. The making of an institution

The most familiar image of Southern slavery reveals the fully-fledged mature institution of the last three decades before the Civil War. A certain timeless, changeless quality has attached itself to that image. But slavery had not always been like that; the "peculiar institution" had its own peculiar history. The slave South was not a fixed point but a changing historical process.

There was nothing clear-cut about the beginnings of slavery on the North American mainland. Blacks were one (but only one) answer to the chronic labour shortage of a colonial society; their status was not established from the outset but clarified over time. The slave trade linked three continents, but South America and the Caribbean were its focal points in the New World, North America little more than an offshoot. Out of some 9,500,000 slaves transported from Africa, only some 427,000 (or 4.5 per cent of the total) were imported into areas which are now part of the United States. Jamaica, Cuba and Haiti each imported many more slaves than the whole of the North American mainland.

The first blacks were brought to Virginia in 1619 – the same year, ironically, in which the first representative assembly in North America, the Virginia House of Burgesses, also first met. Blacks were part of the foundations of American history but their numbers remained very small throughout the seventeenth century. By 1700 there were some 26,000 in the colonies, 70 per cent of them in Virginia and Maryland. Natural increase contributed to rapid growth thereafter, but numbers received their greatest boost during the peak period of slave imports in the mid-eighteenth century. Between 1740 and 1780 over 200,000 slaves were imported – eight times the total black population in 1700. Whereas until the early eighteenth century most slaves came from the West Indies, the great majority during the peak period came direct from Africa. By the time of the American Revolution, there were some half-million slaves, mainly in the southern colonies but with a scattering throughout the Middle Atlantic and New England colonies as well. Slaves formed a higher proportion of the total population in the Revolutionary period than at any other time in American history.

As numbers grew, so too did a clear differentiation of status between slaves and free men. The assumption that the distinction between freedom and servitude must always be clear flows naturally from the attitudes and social structure of modern Western society. However, things looked very different in the European society, shaped by the presence or the legacy of feudalism, from which the settlers came. It is probable that a majority of the seventeenth-century migrants were bound in some form of servitude – most commonly as indentured servants bound to a master for a period of years before obtaining their full freedom. Servant and slave were terms which were interchangeable or at least greatly overlapping.

Much sharper differentiation emerged from the later seventeenth century onwards. On the one hand, attempts to attract more white settlers led to relaxation of the terms of indentured servitude. On the other, particularly for example on the rice plantations of the new colony of South Carolina, a permanent supply of forced labour looked an increasingly attractive proposition. The process of defining a distinct slave status involved the establishment of the principle of servitude for life (and indeed hereditary servitude), and relegation of the slave to the status of mere chattel. Differentiation of status was accompanied by racial differentiation between white and black. Winthrop Jordan has argued persuasively that the institution of chattel slavery and the clear belief in the racial inferiority of the African marched hand in hand, with each supporting and reinforcing the other.[6]

The half century leading to the American Revolution was a period of consolidation and reinforcement of what was now a firmly based institution. Slavery's geographical spread was wide in North as well as South, but its real numerical strength and economic and social importance were still concentrated around its two main Atlantic "bridgeheads", the tobacco-growing area of Virginia and Maryland, and the sub-tropical rice and indigo region of South Carolina and Georgia (see the map on p. vi). In these areas particularly, as slavery strengthened its grip, it evolved its own patterns and routines Blacks imported from Africa had been compelled to adapt to their new surroundings and to the heavy demands of a new way of life. However, by the time of the Revolution the clear majority of the slaves were not Africans but American-born. Most blacks had known no other life but slavery, and masters now had the opportunity to inculcate habits of submissiveness from infancy. The effects of such conditioning from the cradle to the grave were clearly important, although slaves did not necessarily learn from their masters only the lessons which they were intended to learn. Whatever their other methods, slave-owners were never likely to overlook the underlying importance of strict discipline and physical force in controlling their slaves, especially, for example, in South Carolina where slaves constituted 60 per cent of the total population.[7]

Slavery had its embarrassing implications for the ideology, principles and propaganda of the Revolution. However, most revolutionaries, including revolutionary slaveholders, succeeded either in compartmentalizing their thinking, so that the republican liberties of whites could be kept distinct from the emancipation of enslaved blacks, or in reducing the problem to one of priorities and assigning to emancipation a fairly low place. The conservative face of the Revolution showed in a profound respect for property rights, which included property rights in slaves, and in the abiding fear of upsetting the delicate mechanisms of slave society. That conservatism found a new emphasis in the more explicit racism which buttressed the defence of slavery after the Revolution. The free society of the infant republic was a white society. The federal constitution avoided the actual word "slavery" but gave the institution its tacit recognition and protection. The generation of the

Founding Fathers shrank, not surprisingly, from the formidable task of tackling the problem of slavery head on, though it was not averse to attacking its weaker points. Such an approach stored up trouble for the future but, in the meantime, there was comfort in a posture of resigned acceptance of the burdens which the institution laid upon white shoulders, or in the hope that slavery might die of natural causes.

In the event, slavery showed no inclination at all to die, but it was transformed in the forty years from 1790 to 1830. In some respects the peculiar institution gained new strength. Most important of all was the spectacular emergence of cotton as the major staple crop of an expanding South, eager to meet expanding demand. The argument that slavery as a labour system was on its last legs until its salvation by cotton has been shown to be largely myth, but cotton certainly gave slavery an entirely new future, and a new *raison d'être*.

The area of slavery and the number of slaves grew rapidly. From its Upper South and Atlantic seaboard base, slavery spread rapidly into the Deep South. By 1830 the slave population was over two million. The importation of slaves was not prohibited by federal law until 1808 and South Carolina acquired some 40,000 slaves in 1803–07 in the rush to beat the ban, but the main cause of growth was natural increase.

Slavery had demonstrated its capacity to expand and its potential for yet more expansion. But, in the same period, it had also been cribbed and confined in various ways. During or after the Revolution the Northern states all abolished slavery, though the process was painfully slow in some of

11

them. The Northwest Ordinance of 1787 kept slavery out of the vast territory north of the Ohio River – although for more than thirty years attempts were made to break down that barrier. The Missouri Compromise of 1820 barred slavery from most of the huge Louisiana Purchase. The abolition of the slave trade caused anxiety concerning the ability of supply to keep pace with demand for slaves. Mass movement of slaves to the Deep South and Southwest sowed the seeds of slavery's decline in the Upper South. By the 1830s the rising abolitionist movement in the North added moral strictures to the territorial restrictions on slavery.

In 1830 slavery was flourishing as a labour system, a social institution and a device for control of one race by another. But slavery was also fragile and vulnerable.[8] It was a sectional and no longer a national institution: it was exceptional – an unmistakably peculiar institution which set the South apart not only from the North but from almost the entire Atlantic world; it was an uneasy institution, sensitive to outside attack and disturbed by uncertainties within. It was a system which lived on, by and with fear. Slaves were conditioned to fear their masters; non-slaveowning whites felt threatened socially and economically by blacks, whether slave or free; all Southern whites shared the constant, nagging fear of servile insurrection. The whole white South feared outside interference or domination. The slaveowners feared for their social status, their economic well-being and their personal security, should their peculiar institution come to an end. Indeed, the fear which subsumed so many others was dread of the consequences – economic ruin, social chaos and racial anarchy – which, it was generally believed, would follow the abandonment of slavery.

Two prominent features of Southern slavery conspired to add to the paradoxes of the system. First, it was explicitly and essentially racial slavery. The line of race and colour drawn between master and slave was so firm that the few exceptions to it did not threaten it. This line dictated the formal rigidity of the master–slave relationship. The difficulty and the rarity of manumission, and the twilight existence of the free black community. There were few escape hatches of any kind, and the colour of a slave's skin marked him indelibly. Bondage was a life sentence and a hereditary one. Elkins attributes the harsh lines and the severity of this slave system to its origins in "unrestrained capitalism", systematic exploitation by highly individualist capitalist enterprise, unmitigated by the mediating influence of a powerful church or aristocracy or monarchy as in Latin America.[9] Elkins may exaggerate the differences between North and South American styles of slavery, but they did exist. However, racism rather than capitalism may have been the villain of the piece.

The other unquestionable – indeed unique – distinctive mark of slavery in the Southern states was the natural increase of the slave population. In all other slave societies of the New World, the slave population failed to reproduce itself and was sustained or increased only by constant injection of new slaves from Africa. In Latin America, and especially in the Caribbean, the system was one of rapid and ruthless exploitation of the slaves to the point of exhaustion, sickness and death, and their replacement by fresh stock. In the Southern colonies and later states, of North America, the demographic pattern was quite different, partly perhaps because the ravages of infectious diseases were less severe, and partly because there was less voracious demand for the products of the eighteenth-century South than for West Indian sugar, and therefore less temptation to seek high profits by ruthless exploitation (and exhaustion) of the labour force.[10] In contrast to the heavy male preponderance in slave populations elsewhere, there was a near balance of the sexes which, for almost a century before 1808, was already producing a natural increase. After the abolition of the external slave trade in that year, the South depended on its own resources for future slave manpower. Whether or not they had fully realized it before, it was now clearly in the interest of slaveholders to provide at least the minimal material and social conditions which would foster (or, at least, not discourage) slave fertility.

The juxtaposition of these two features – rigidity and harshness on the one hand, a measure of concern for slave living standards on the other – helps to explain one of the inner contradictions of the whole system. Southern slavery sought to combine two apparently incompatible elements. It totally denied any rights to the slave, aimed to reduce him to a state of total dependence, and tried to enclose him completely and inescapably within the system. Yet, at the same time, it made material provision for the slave superior to that provided by other systems of bondage, moderated the severity of the system in its practical day-by-day application, made room for an element of paternalism in the master–slave relationship, and used the mediating influence of tacit compromise and "doublethink". The slave society of the double standard was the product of a very distinctive historical and demographic background.

3. The labour of the slaves

There is a growing awareness among historians of the importance of the earlier history of slavery in North America, but it remains true that our knowledge and understanding of the peculiar institution are greatest in its last few decades, and this pamphlet is mainly concerned with slavery in its maturity. The census of 1860 showed that there were nearly four million slaves out of a total population of 12,300,000 in the fifteen slave states. The proportion of slave to white population varied greatly from area to area. In South Carolina and Mississippi more than half the population were slaves, and in Louisiana, Alabama, Florida and Georgia more than two-fifths. In no other state did slaves amount to one-third of the population; in Maryland the proportion was 13 per cent, in Missouri 10 per cent, in Delaware a mere 1.5 per cent.

Overall, there were some 385,000 slaveowners out of about one and a half million white families (and a total white population of eight million). Fifty per cent of slaveowners owned no more than five slaves, and only 12 per cent owned twenty or more. At the summit of the Southern social pyramid were the 10,000 owners with more than fifty slaves, including 3,000 with more than one hundred. The majority of slaveholders were therefore small-scale owners, but the large-scale ownership of a small minority meant that more than half the slaves lived on plantations with more than twenty slaves. At the two extremes were the 25 per cent of slaves on plantations with more than fifty, and another 25 per cent in units of less than ten.

The underlying theme of these statistics is the variety of slavery in terms of location, distribution of population and size of unit of ownership. Behind all these figures lies the fundamental but forgettable fact that three quarters of Southern white families owned no slaves at all. Numerically at least, the typical white Southerner was a small farmer, cultivating his own soil and not unlike his Northern counterpart, except that he lived cheek-by-jowl with slavery, and accepted its social and racial imperatives as well as its economic repercussions.

The great majority of slaves were employed in agriculture or occupations relating to it. However, there was considerable variety in the nature and organization of work. The working life of slaves of smaller owners was not in many respects very different from the lot of the farm labourer elsewhere. The owner commonly worked alongside his bondsmen in the fields and the working relationship, indeed the whole way of life, was obviously less organized and formalized than on the plantation. "I have no overseer," wrote one such farmer, "and do not manage so scientifically as those who are able to lay down rules; yet I endeavor to manage so that myself, family and negroes may take pleasure and delight in our relations."[11] Much less has been said and written about slavery in this kind of environment than on the large plantation. It is the great planters who have left much the most substantial historical record.

Among plantation slaves probably no more than half were full-time field hands. The remainder were full-time or part-time domestics, craftsmen, mechanics, gardeners, blacksmiths, millers, seamstresses or general handymen. The relentless routine of the seasons required more labour in the fields at some times, less at others. But it was man-made routine which dictated the working life of a plantation. Hours were long – traditionally from sun-up to sundown – but recognized breaks during the day were generally observed as were holidays at such times as Christmas, and slaves as well as free men rested on the Sabbath.

Although slaves were employed in general, mixed farming, most worked on the cultivation of the great staple crops of the South. The census of 1850 offered estimates (which may be little more than reasonable guesses) of the numbers of slaves employed in the production of staple crops. Out of 2,500,000 slaves directly employed in agriculture, it calculated that 350,000 were engaged in production of tobacco, 150,000 in sugar, 125,000 in rice, 60,000 in hemp and a massive 1,815,000 in cotton.

The organization and supervision of a substantial slave workforce demanded considerable management skill. The subject was endlessly debated in the Southern press. An owner of up to thirty slaves would probably have supervised them himself, with help from his family. The more complex operation of a larger plantation generally required the services of an overseer. He was the man between master and slaves, an intermediary or a mediator used but not always trusted by either side. If the size of the workforce justified it, the overseer would have slave drivers under him, each of whom normally supervised the work of a slave gang. Masters and overseers classified their slaves as full or fractional (half, quarter, etc.) hands, with the old, the younger children, expectant and nursing mothers regarded as equivalent to something less than a full field hand.

A number of issues relating to the work of slaves have excited historical controversy. How hard did slaves in fact work? What were the relative roles of sanctions and rewards in forcing or persuading slaves to work hard? Was slave labour efficient? The view long prevailed that slaves worked long and hard because they were forced to, under the threat of the lash, but that they achieved no high level of efficiency. Low efficiency was made tolerable by the low cost of slave labour. Stampp's interpretation belongs broadly to this school of thought, but he also offers a balanced appraisal of the role of incentives – a garden plot, permission to sell produce from it, extra holidays or passes to leave the plantation, and even money payments and crude profit-sharing schemes. But he sees incentives as but one weapon (and a subsidiary one) in an armoury of slave control which included firm discipline, demonstration of the master's power (symbolized by the whip), and the inculcation of a sense of inferiority.[12]

Current debate on this as on so many issues centres around Fogel and Engerman's remarkable conclusions in their highly controversial book *Time on the Cross*. Their case for the efficiency of the slave system depends heavily not only upon the advantages of organization and manipulation of a large labour force but on the superior quality of the workforce itself. Slaves, they argue, were not lazy and inept but on average more efficient and industrious than their white counterparts. Their masters had not merely organized them effectively but had imbued them with the Protestant work ethic, a drive towards self-improvement by their own efforts.

The superiority of slave workers was not, according to Fogel and Engerman, the result of abnormally long hours, constant and brutal punishment or ruthless exploitation. In their estimation, slaves worked shorter hours and fewer days in the year than contemporary free workers, the extent of whipping has been grossly exaggerated, and slaves received as "income" (though not of course a cash income) something like 90 per cent of the product of their labour. A mere 10 per cent rate of expropriation by their owners compared favourably with what other employers took from their wage-earning employees.

In the *Time on the Cross* version of slavery, the carrot replaces the stick, though not completely. Fogel and Engerman suggest that the kind of incentives described by Stampp and others were far more widely offered than was previously thought. But they go further in claiming that, in the ranks of slave labour there was a hierarchy which was tantamount to a career structure. An industrious and co-operative slave might be "promoted" to one of a variety of skilled occupations, or to a supervisory position as a driver or even an overseer. The slaves were not brutalized but socialized.[13]

In *Reckoning with Slavery*, the most comprehensive counterblast to *Time on the Cross*, Herbert Gutman and

Richard Sutch have set out to rebut this case point by point, with a degree of success that most would agree is considerable and many might think decisive. The basic criticism is that the conclusions of *Time on the Cross* are derived from the rigid application of a model rather than the use of specific evidence and that such evidence as is cited, on whipping for example, is slender, untypical, and often misunderstood. The lash was used more often than Fogel and Engerman allow, and the number of "promoted posts" available to slaves far smaller than they claim. More fundamental is the danger of arguing backwards from consequences to causes. A hierarchy of jobs is not the same as a career structure. Its existence does not prove that it was being systematically used as an incentive scheme.[14]

Moreover, a widespread use of rewards and incentives would not in itself prove that coercion was unimportant in making slaves work hard. Surely in a slave system, force or the threat of force is fundamental and all other methods are secondary. Of course planters used techniques of persuasion, mediation and compromise, including rewards and payments, but only within the basic coercive framework. They did so for sound economic reasons, but for other reasons too. It was often easier and more convenient to tread softly. It made for a quieter life and it avoided, in the daily routine, pushing the logic of slavery to its extremes of inhumanity. But it was only the presence or the threat of coercion which permitted the use of persuasion Coercion could be relaxed if, and only as long as, gentler measures worked. It is possible to turn against Fogel and Engerman a quotation which they use from a set of instructions to plantation managers:

The object of all punishment should be, 1st, for correction to deter the offender from the repetition of an offence, from the fear of the like certain punishment; and, 2nd, for example to all others, shewing them that if they offend, they will likewise receive certain punishment. And these objects and ends of all just punishments can be better attained by the certainty than by the severity of punishment.[15]

Punishment served as deterrent and as example to others. If it continued to serve its purpose without constant application, all well and good. But infrequent resort to the exercise of a power may testify to its importance and effectiveness rather than the opposite. Rewards and incentives were the superstructure built upon the foundations of coercion.

In one of the most oft-quoted passages in his accounts of his travels in the slave South, Frederick Law Olmsted commented upon the discipline and concentration of a large hoe gang at work in the fields. In Time on the Cross the quoted passage ends as follows:

I repeatedly rode through the lines at a canter, with other horsemen, often coming upon them suddenly, without producing the smallest change or interruption in the dogged action of the labourers, or causing one of them, so far as I could see, to lift an eye from the ground.

In *Reckoning with Slavery*, the critics take Fogel and Engerman to task, rightly, for omitting the next sentence:

A very tall and powerful negro walked to and fro in the rear of the line, frequently cracking his whip, and calling out, in the surliest manner, to one and another, "Shove your hoe, there! Shove your hoe."

Unfortunately, the critics spoil a good point by themselves omitting the short sentence which follows:

But I never saw him strike any one with the whip.[16]

The full extract reveals much more about the nature of slave control than any one piece of it carefully selected to serve as ammunition for historical controversy.

Slave labour involved not only the coercion but the exploitation of the slave. It has been demonstrated that the owner's "rate of expropriation" of the fruits of the slave's labour was not the 10 (or possibly 12) per cent calculated by Fogel and Engerman, but probably nearer to 50 per cent.[17] Again evidence offered in *Time on the Cross* can supply unintended clues to the existence of a system of harsh exploitation. For example, in seeking to explain why the demand for slave labour in agriculture was inelastic – that is, why free labour did not compete with it – Fogel and Engerman concede that even if planters had been able to offer small white farmers wages 50 per cent above their normal earnings they would not have been tempted to form themselves into a labour gang. The reason lay in the "negative nonpecuniary income" of slave workers.[18] Negative nonpecuniary income means in plain language that the work was unpleasant and unattractive to a degree which could not be overcome, in the eyes of free workers, even by large financial inducements. Free men would not voluntarily undertake work which slaves were compelled to do.

Again, Fogel and Engerman refer to "the extraordinarily high labour participation rate" of the plantation workforce. This meant that "virtually every slave capable of being in the labor force was in it." In the tree labour system about one-third of the total population was in the workforce. In the slave system the proportion was two-thirds.[19] The reason was simply that women and children, the aged and the handicapped were all required to work. This was the result of compulsion, not incentives. Moreover, they were made to work very intensively under constant supervision. Contrary to the estimates in *Time on the Cross*, and allowing for the hazards of all such comparisons, many authorities support the conventional view that slaves also worked longer hours and had fewer days off, even than nineteenth-century industrial workers, and certainly than free blacks did after the Civil War. Slave labour was both intensive and extensive.

A different perspective on the work of slaves may be found in the work of Eugene Genovese, even if there is some risk of jumping out of the cliometrical frying-pan into the ideological fire. Genovese, a Marxist historian much influenced by the Italian thinker Antonio Gramsci, is no simplistic evangelist for the gospel of economic determinism. In his major work, *Roll, Jordan, Roll: the World the Slaves Made*, he has used the concepts of paternalism and hegemony on the master's side, and the complex balance between accommodation and resistance on the slave's side, to build up an elaborate picture of the web of interdependence between owner and owned. Genovese injects class as well as race into his analysis of the slave system, and depicts the slave's attitude to his master and to his work as a variant of the class struggle under capitalism. However, the foreground of Genovese's picture of slave life and work carries conviction, with or without the ideological background.

"The slaveholders," says Genovese, "presided over a plantation system that constituted a halfway house between peasant and factory cultures." They sought to impose upon their slaves a discipline and an attitude to work which the system required but which they did not admire or practise themselves. The slaves sought to defend themselves as best they could against an enforced system of exploitation and an imposed set of values. "The plantation system served as a halfway house for Africans between their agricultural past and their imposed industrial future." The slaveholders "had their way, but paid a price" in concessions to the slaves. Much more persuasively than Fogel and Engerman, Genovese describes the balance between coercion and persuasion in the slave system. He recognizes that slaves often did co-operate and respond to incentives, but he shows a sensitivity to the compromises and contradictions required to cope with the problems of daily life which entirely eludes the authors of *Time on the Cross*. There is a sense of history and of the human predicament in the one work which is missing in the other.

In Genovese's view, slaves could and did work hard, but they resented the regularity and routine which the system imposed. They could be goaded or encouraged into special effort at peak periods of the year, and found some fulfilment and heightened sense of community in such common exertion. However, for most slaves it was difficult to relate the toil which occupied most of their waking hours to the satisfaction of personal and family needs. They were not paid, and their rewards seemed in no way commensurate with the quantity or quality of their labour. They usually lacked the satisfaction as well as the responsibilities of a wage-earner.[20] There were, however, some exceptions to this rule; a sense of involvement and even satisfaction in one's work was possible in the case of some skilled plantation slaves, for example, or of some industrial slaves who developed attitudes and accepted responsibilities (and discovered opportunities) which encouraged them to remain in the same occupations when emancipation came.[21]

Slave work is central to the study of slave society. It leads directly to consideration of even broader issues, on the one hand the overall efficiency and profitability of the slave economy of the South, and on the other the quality of slave life, the nature of the slave personality and the development of slave culture. These problems are the subject of the next two sections.

4. The business of slavery

The economic performance of slavery was affected by all kinds of factors, social and racial, moral and personal, political and psychological. The obvious yardstick of economic performance is profitability, but initially discussion of the profitability of slavery raises more questions than it answers.[22] The most obvious question is simply: profitable for whom? The answer depends on whether slavery is considered as a business or a system. If the first, one must ask whether it was profitable for individuals, groups, and interests involved in it – the slaveholders (obviously), the slaves themselves (less obviously but necessarily in the post-*Time on the Cross* debate), merchants and middlemen, and, in a slightly different sense, the consumers of its products. On the second point – slavery as a system – one must ask whether the community or society as a whole benefited from slavery. Did the economy of the South gain or lose by it?

The next vital distinction is between absolute and relative profitability. On the one hand, the question may simply be whether, on average, slaveowners made a profit or a loss. In Stampp's sensible formulation, did the average ante-bellum slaveholder over the years earn a reasonably satisfactory return from his investment? On the other hand, the question may be whether he could have made a greater profit by dispensing with slavery and using his resources differently. Similarly, for the South as a whole, there is a distinction between the question "did the South gain or lose by slavery?" and the question "could the South have done better without slavery?" Was the alleged "backwardness" of the South a consequence of its addiction to slave labour?

The fundamental priorities of slavery are involved here. If slavery was above all else a rational economic system devoted to the pursuit of profit, those who controlled it would have retained their investment in it only if it continued to show greater profit than alternative forms of enterprise. However, if slavery was even more important as an instrument of social and racial adjustment, its masters may have been content to maintain it for those reasons alone, as long as it did not prove cripplingly unprofitable. It seems likely that if slaveholders could have read the refined, complicated and somewhat esoteric arguments deployed in the modern debate over the economics of slavery, many would have found them unimpressive and even irrelevant (not to say unintelligible).

The economic fortunes of slavery fluctuated between one time or place or, indeed, one person and another. It was subject to booms and slumps like almost any other business. Its profits (and the methods of making them) differed between the Upper South and the Lower South or the Atlantic seaboard and the lower Mississippi valley, or between cotton and sugar plantations. They varied obviously too from one owner to another, according to his business acumen, his social aspirations, his intelligence and his luck, not to mention the site of his farm or plantation and the quality of his land. Profitability still depended on individual ability.

One more vital distinction remains. Profitability and efficiency are not quite the same thing. Profit may result, and often does result, from efficiency, but it may also arise from other causes – ruthless and extravagant exploitation of forced labour or virgin land, or a monopoly or near-monopoly position as supplier of a product in urgent demand.

When all the appropriate qualifications have been made, there remains no doubt that many slaveowners made reasonable (and sometimes handsome) profits in the pre-Civil War years. Most authorities agree that they received a return upon their investment which was in line with, if not superior to, that available elsewhere. Such a finding clearly undermines the old view of Phillips and others that slavery often laid a burden of unprofitability upon the planters which they shouldered because they supported the institution for other reasons. However, it does not follow that because slavery yielded a good return, profit was the only motive and ambition of slaveholders. The slaveowner was not necessarily a capitalist pure and simple, just because he happened to make money.

The current debate focuses once again on Fogel and Engerman, although it is worth noting the extent to which Stampp prefigured some of the more sober conclusions of *Time on the Cross*. Fogel and Engerman maintain that the profitability of the business of slavery derived from the efficiency of Southern slave agriculture, which they attribute to good management, a high-quality work force, and the economies of scale slavery made possible. They even claim that Southern agriculture was more efficient than Northern, and place a precise figure of 35 per cent upon the margin of superiority. This figure is derived from the "geometric index of total factor productivity", through which efficiency is measured by the ratio of output to the average amount of the inputs of land, labour and capital.[23]

However, their case rests on an unrealistic and ultimately false comparison. For all its cliometric ingenuity, it is surely impossible to make a fair and illuminating comparison between a large-scale planter with fifty or one hundred slaves, producing cotton for export, and the characteristic Northern small family farm employing little if any labour outside the family, and yielding a variety of cereal and animal products. The two operations are different in scale, structure and purpose and in their social and economic context. There was nothing in Northern agriculture comparable to the Southern cotton plantation.

Two of the factors in the geometric index – land on the input side, cotton on the output side – illustrate the hazards of attempts to compare like with unlike. Northern land values were generally higher, partly because transportation routes and urban-industrial development were more advanced than in the South. The Northern input of land was therefore higher in money terms than the Southern, and the ratio of output to inputs therefore lower, if the index is rigidly and misleadingly followed. Fogel and Engerman are unrepentant on this point and the debate continues, but the objection must surely lead to some modification, though not necessarily abandonment, of their position.

The second objection, concerning cotton, is more fundamental. Gavin Wright has developed the alternative hypothesis that the insatiable demand for cotton, and the quantity and quality of cotton-growing land in the South, hold the key to the high productivity and profitability of Southern slave agriculture. Furthermore, reliance on the evidence of the census of 1860 has greatly exaggerated the "efficiency" of Southern agriculture, for 1859–60 was a time of unparalleled boom for cotton producers. The profits of Southern planters owed less to the efficiency of slave labour than to being in the right place at the right time to satisfy an exceptional demand.[24] This does not of course mean that slave-based agriculture was inefficient and unprofitable; it does call into question the superior efficiency claimed for it, and the explanation of that superiority. At the very least it does not follow that, because Southern agriculture used slave labour and because it showed a profit, its profits were the result of its labour system and nothing else. The authors of *Time on the Cross* may quite simply have backed the wrong horse.

Some of the same considerations recur in attempts to assess the profitability of the slave system to the South as a whole. It was perfectly possible, of course, for slavery to be a good business proposition for slaveholders but a poor economic proposition for the South in general. It is fairly obvious that it did not promote the economic well-being of various non-slaveowning sections of the community – and the non-slaveowners were the large majority of the white population. There were wide disparities in wealth in the

31

South which reflected the gap between the great planters and the poorer whites. The latter lived in constant dread of the day when they might have to compete with freed slaves, but in fact they were suffering all the time from wage levels depressed by slave competition. Slavery was a rich man's joy but a poor man's plight.

If it is the cotton boom which holds the key, parts of the South felt the strain of sharing only indirectly in it, and it can be argued that slavery was a declining institution in parts of the border states and the Upper South before the Civil War. It was long believed – and this view was reinforced by the pioneering cliometric work of Conrad and Meyer – that those areas boosted their flagging fortunes by selling their surplus slaves to the Deep South. Some historians talk of or hint at, slavebreeding as an organized business. Fogel and Engerman have derided the conventional view of the scale and economic importance of the domestic slave trade. They suggest that, although there was a forced migration of several hundred thousand slaves across the South in the pre-Civil War decades, most of them were not sold but either moved with their owners or were sent by them to their new lands in the West. However, this line of argument has been shattered, and its slender basis in the evidence laid bare, by Sutch and Gutman.[25] Precise conclusions on this subject are difficult but it seems clear enough that slave sales were numerically significant, and economically important to the Upper South. The question of slavebreeding for sale depends on one's definition of terms. Systematic breeding of slaves for market was unusual. The slave stud-farm no doubt existed but it was exceptional. However, owners were well aware of the marketability of their slaves, and fecundity added to the value of a young female slave. It would be fair to say that slaveholders exploited the fertility of their slaves but seldom sought to increase it by forced mating. They enjoyed the profits of coition without coercion.

As for the economic "backwardness" of the South, so many factors are involved that it is virtually impossible to isolate the retarding effect, if any, of slavery alone. There is a strong presumption that slavery imposed a certain rigidity and inflexibility upon the Southern economy, that the dead weight of the slave system prevented the South from seizing new opportunities, that low levels of literacy and skill inhibited economic growth, and that the depressed living standards of many Southerners, white and black, reduced the consumer capacity of the home market.

On the other hand, when the Civil War came, slavery and the economic system based upon it were certainly not in any imminent danger of collapse through inefficiency or unprofitability. Arguments that agriculture based on slave labour necessarily led to soil exhaustion or that slavery and industry were incompatible have been shown to belong to the realm of myth rather than fact. Whatever its problems, slavery had demonstrated its flexibility and its resilience as a labour system. The fact that the South lagged behind the North in urban-industrial development can be interpreted as testimony to the health, not the sickness, of the Southern slave economy. Perhaps the very success (and the profits) of plantation slavery and cotton production removed any incentive to switch from agriculture to industrial or urban development. Slavery had proved its capacity, it is argued, to adapt to factories and cities, but at the peaks of the cotton boom, slaves were actually drawn out of the towns and on to the plantations because they could be more profitably used there. In towns they could be replaced by white immigrant workers; on the plantation they were irreplaceable.[26]

There is a wider point about Southern "backwardness". In one of their more intriguing comparative ventures, Fogel and Engerman suggest that, in terms of the level of per capita income, the Southern states would have ranked fourth in the world in 1860, behind only Australia, the northern United States and Great Britain, and that the rate of increase of per capita income was faster in the South than the North.[27] Of course, the cotton boom might be used to explain the high place of the South in this league table relative to most European countries. But the figure for the South was still only 73 per cent of that for the North in 1860. However, Fogel and Engerman go on to separate the Northeastern states from the North Central. They then show that the level of *per capita* income was 14 per cent lower in the North Central states than in the South. Again, perhaps cotton gave the South the advantage. But the crucial point is surely that it is the Northeast which enjoyed an enormous lead over the South, presumably because of its urban-industrial development. The effect of slavery, whether by its success or its failure, in inhibiting such development in the South must surely have more to answer for than the authors of *Time on the Cross* will allow.

Gavin Wright makes the point very effectively in a different way by distinguishing between growth and development. The Southern economy grew extensively while the Northern economy diversified, urbanized and industrialized. Development in the North fostered the

Slavery also had a Northern face. This remarkable
daguerrotype, taken by an unknown photographer about
1850, is said to be of Ceasar, the last slave owned in New
York. Though an act for gradual emancipation was passed in
that state in 1799, the process was not completed until 1841,
and even then non-residents were allowed, down to 1841, to
have slaves with them while visiting the state.

process of sustained economic growth. In contrast, the South enjoyed the ephemeral advantage of being the dominant supplier of the world market for cotton, a position which offered short-run enjoyment of profit not necessarily linked to real efficiency, but not the long-term prospect of sustained growth.[28] Perhaps, after all, the argument leads us back to the conclusion of Lewis C. Gray, who some forty years ago saw in slavery "the near-paradox of an economic institution competitively effective under certain conditions, but essentially regressive in its influence on the socio-economic evolution of the section where it prevailed."[29]

Profitability may have been a valuable lubricant of the slave system rather than its propellant fuel. White Southerners, whether slave-holders or not, adhered to slavery above all because it was there, and they dreaded the consequences of its demise. Slave and master were locked together in a system which the one could not escape and the other would not abandon.

5. The life of the slaves

Phrases like "the slave experience", "the slave personality", "slave culture" have become part of the common currency of all discussion of the subject. Inevitably they mean different things to different people, and their free and easy use (even in the hands of able and sympathetic historians) comes close at times to denying to slaves even a share of the varieties of experience, the vagaries of personality and the diversity of culture which other men are assumed to have. The attempt to achieve some understanding of slave life involves digging through several layers of formative influences: material living conditions, the physical environment, the psychological impact of generations of bondage, the personal factors in the master–slave relationship, the survivals of an African heritage, the pervading influence of white American society.

The material standards of slave life were modest, but generally above the level of bare survival. Much depended on the character of the master and on his circumstances. It was obviously in his interest to provide a certain very basic level of care and maintenance. Failure to do so in some cases may have indicated ignorance rather than ill-will. Masters and slaves lived in an age of low standards in diet, hygiene, public health and medical skill. Slaves had a lower life expectancy than Southern whites but the difference was not large. According to the 1860 census, 3.5 per cent of the slave population was over sixty years of age, compared with 4.4 per cent of the whites. There is certainly ample evidence that, although there was a very high birth-rate among slaves, infant mortality was also very high – perhaps even twice as high as among whites.

The diet of most slaves was probably adequate, even bulky, but dull and, in some respects, nutritionally deficient. In this, as in its emphasis on "hogs and hominy", it resembled the diet of many Southern whites. Some slaves were able to supplement their basic rations with the products of their own garden plots or hunting and fishing expeditions – or raids upon the master's smoke-house or poultry-yard. Slave housing varied considerably in quality and character, between small farms and larger plantations – and between one plantation and another, but in most cases the slave quarters consisted of a group of wooden cabins, huddled in a group not too near and not too far from the big house.

The living conditions of slaves have become the subject of yet another major controversy. *Time on the Cross* adopts the view that diet and housing and health were not unreasonable by the standards of the time, but its arguments are again flawed by overstatements and misleading comparisons. A single example, concerning housing, must suffice. It is suggested in *Time on the Cross* that a typical slave cabin measured twenty feet by eighteen and that there was an average of 5.2 persons per cabin. This compared favourably, it is claimed with the housing of free workers, and specifically with the results of a survey of working-class housing in New York City in 1893, which estimated the median area of sleeping space per person at thirty-five square feet, roughly half the average for the slave cabin. Sutch has subjected these figures to devastating scrutiny, and produces an entirely different picture. The twenty feet by eighteen feet cabin was near an ideal standard suggested by articles in Southern journals; fifteen feet square would be nearer the true average. The average number of persons per cabin was not 5.2 but over six. The New York survey covered, not typical working-class housing, but a small sample of the worst slum areas, in the first year of a severe depression. The median area of thirty-five square feet referred to sleeping space not living space. *Time on the Cross* compares the whole slave cabin to the bedroom space in the New York apartments, the majority of which had at least three rooms. The final twist to the story is that the New York survey dealt not with floor area but cubic capacity and Fogel and Engerman "converted" this figure to floor space by allowing a somewhat generous ceiling height of eleven feet![30] Until the statistical evidence becomes more trustworthy, more conventional sources must be relied upon to bring us back to the real world of rickety, unpainted, cramped slave quarters, with earth floors and windows without glass, swept by draughts in winter, stifling in the summer heat, choking with smoke, or swarming with insects.

However, it is not the physical environment but the psychological impact of slavery which has become the great historiographical battlefield. Elkins argues that the severity of the slave regime in the Southern states crippled the slave personality, but he is very clear that it was not material deprivation but the overall impact of a tightly-closed system which inflicted the damage. In his view it created Sambo – docile but irresponsible, loyal but lazy, humble but deceitful – the stereotype of the American slave. In effect, the Elkins thesis replaced the old concept of the racial inferiority of the black slave with the new concept of psychological handicap or damage, inflicted by the total institution of slavery. The first explained the personality problems of the Negro slave by his negritude, the second by his servitude. The vigorous reaction against Elkins in the last twenty years has encouraged a third view of a distinct Afro-American personality, in no way inferior, but forged and tempered in the furnace of slavery.

The Elkins thesis is impressive in its coherence and its logic. The shock of enslavement detached the slave from his old society and his old self; the total institution of slavery fastened new standards and a new personality upon him. The authority of his new master was so massive as to produce child-like dependence and conformity. Using the insights of interpersonal theory and role psychology, Elkins argues that all lines led back to the master because of the lack of "significant others" – other people with the authority and influence to affect the slave personality. The slave therefore internalized the attitudes and standards of this sole significant other. Similarly, according to role psychology, the personality develops through playing a number of different social roles as child, parent, husband, friend, worker, learner, patient, purchaser, and so on. However, under slavery there was only one all-pervading role which produced complete dependence and submissiveness.

The whole Elkins argument rests on the psychological impact of "closed systems" or total institutions. It is in this context that he introduces the highly controversial analogy between Southern slavery and the Nazi concentration camp. Evidence from the camps showed in the starkest form the capacity of a total institution to produce drastic personality change. What such camps could do in a few years, says Elkins, slavery could surely do in a few generations.[31]

Elkins' thesis was vulnerable partly because the elegance of his theoretical model was not matched by detailed investigation of the realities of slavery as it actually existed. Perhaps his greatest success has been in the quality of the response which he has evoked. The clarity and the audacity of his argument stimulated a wealth of new insights and ideas, most of them sharply critical. The concentration-camp analogy was a virtual invitation to counter-attack as well as to misrepresentation. While the notion of a closed system offers valuable insights into slavery, it is widely felt that, on any scale of "total institutions", the concentration camp and the slave plantation would stand at opposite ends. (Some are more total than others!) The plantation was a place of life and work, the camp a systematic instrument of death, with a mortality rate sometimes running at 20 per cent per month. Elkins also plays down the evidence that, even amid the unimaginable horrors of the concentration camp, there were inmates who did not totally submit or collapse, who did not conform to the model. Questions have also been raised about the Sambo stereotype itself. It may be hard to distinguish, as Elkins himself admits, where

41

the true personality ends and the play-acting begins, but it seems clear that many slaves played the Sambo role either to avoid work or trouble, or to conform to what was expected of them. Blassingame speaks of "ritual deference", particularly among domestic slaves. However, Sambo was probably more than simply a white invention or a black performance. Totally submissive slaves of this type existed but they represented only one possible response among many to the pressures of bondage. Different slaves responded in diverse ways, and the same slave responded differently as situations changed – and as masters changed, too, for slaves commonly had experience of more than one owner. Blassingame describes the typical field hand as "sullenly obedient and hostilely submissive",[32] a description less tidy but more plausible than the out-and-out Sambo. Slave personality and slave behaviour were not set in any one mould. The variety of approaches, mixing coercion and persuasion, which were pursued in the practical management of slaves suggests some measure of white recognition of variations in slave personality. It is ironical that the rewards and encouragements offered to slaves, which Fogel and Engerman see as part of an elaborate scheme of work incentives, may have been devices to relieve some of the inner tensions of slavery rather than to increase slave work rate. They were often tranquillizers rather than stimuli, safety-valves rather than incentives.

Elkins also exaggerated the picture of the master as the only "significant other" in the life of the slave. There were many "others" of varying significance from members of the owner's family and other nearby whites to the slave's own family and neighbours in the slave quarters. Elkins badly underestimates the separate life of the slave community because he overestimates the totality of the closed system of slavery. In fact it left significant spaces which the slaves were able to fill themselves. In this, the plantation may resemble the prison, the hospital, the army camp (or the boarding school?) much more closely than the concentration camp. Elkins has admitted the force of the criticisms of Fredrickson and Lasch, Bryce-Laporte and others, and has retreated a little from what appeared to many to be his original all-or-nothing position. If the closed system is not quite so closed after all, the way is open to recognition of a different, more complex master-slave relationship, and a richer life within the slave community itself. "Something less than absolute power," he writes, "produces something less than absolute dependency."[33]

On the whole, slaves did not come to terms with their situation in one big, final decision to accept or reject the system. Abject submission was one extreme, violent rebellion the other, and the overwhelming majority of slaves established a pattern of behaviour in the broad area between the two. Slave rebellions were infrequent and ill-starred because the odds were so heavily against them. All the instruments of power were in white hands, the problems of communication and co-ordination involved in planning a large-scale revolt were immense, and the slaves did not enjoy in most parts of the South the huge numerical advantage which they had possessed in other parts of the New World. Moreover, the evolving life of the slave community and the slave family created ties and responsibilities which inhibited thoughts of outright rebellion and obliged the slave to consider what he had to lose. The same restraints limited but did not stop individual flight from slavery. Here the difficulty was not so much in running away as in evading recapture. The odds against a successful escape to the North were great and most fugitives were caught within days. Some slaves were habitual runaways, and some took flight as a kind of ritual gesture of defiance or as a reaction to punishment.

Less dramatic than rebellion or flight were the various forms of sabotage, disruption, obstruction, non-co-operation, and malingering which were woven into the pattern of slave life. Slaves feigned ignorance or illness, worked carelessly, broke tools, damaged or set fire to property, and stole from their masters. The line between a natural desire to avoid hard work and a more deliberate intention to protest or resist was no doubt often hard to draw. Fredrickson and Lasch doubt whether most such actions can be called resistance, because for them resistance is a political concept which implies some planned, violent action. They prefer the term non-co-operation. Levine observes that the slaves did not oppose slavery "politically" because they were a "pre-political" people who did not think in terms of political institutions or organized, concerted action as vehicles for protest and opposition, but who resisted in other ways, whether through various forms of passive resistance or through drawing upon spiritual and cultural resources which enabled them to transcend the temporal bonds of slavery. Genovese makes a similar point. The combination of paternalism and racism, he says, kept the slaves from full appreciation of their individual and – more important – their collective strength. They had not learned to act like political men.[34]

Twentieth-century minds may well find difficulty in appreciating the "slave's eye view" of slavery, and the perceptions and priorities which followed from it. Notions of security and insecurity, for example, must have been transformed by experience of slavery. In some respects the slave enjoyed a large measure of "security", if not a very agreeable one. He did not have the worry or the responsibility of providing food, shelter and clothing for himself and his family, or of providing for old age, or of searching for employment. There was a peculiar sense of security and order in being enveloped in a system which governed all such aspects of life and which made decisions upon them. On the other hand, the slave suffered the terrible insecurity of the threat of sale which might break up his family, or of punishment and harsh treatment which could humiliate and degrade him. His personal and domestic life were at the mercy of his master's whim. In such a topsy-turvy world, the slave had to balance the urge to resist against the demands of simple survival.

Genovese may tend to exaggerate the explicit and conscious element in the striking of such a balance. At times his description resembles the formal, ritualized processes of bargaining in modern labour relations. However, no one has presented a more convincing picture of the character, and the compromises, of the master–slave relationship. "The slaves," he says, "had turned the dependency relationship to their own limited advantage ... Out of necessity they had made an uneven agreement but it was nonetheless an agreement." Breakdowns or betrayals of that agreement could lead to eruptions of violence, but, in general, "the slaves' acceptance of paternalism ... signaled acceptance of an imposed white domination within which they drew their own lines, asserted rights, and preserved their self-respect."[35] In the words of an ex-slave, "white folks do as they please, and the darkies do as they can."[36]

By doing as they could, enslaved blacks fostered a life style of their own, a distinct slave culture. Was slave culture largely a response to the impact of slavery itself? The traditional affirmative answer is re-stated, for example, by Joel Williamson: "Most of what constituted black culture was a survival response to the world the white man made; now blacks had to shape their lives largely within the round of possibilities generated by whites."[37] In *The Black Family in Slavery and Freedom*, however, Herbert Gutman has vigorously attacked this view, and charged most of the leading historians of slavery with complicity in its propagation. He emphasizes the way in which slave culture developed through the cumulative experience of generations and from the inner resources of the slave community. It was an adaptive process to the rigours of slavery, but the form of that adaptation was shaped from within. He agrees with Sidney Mintz and Richard Price that Afro-American slave institutions "took on their characteristic shape *within* the parameters of the master's monopoly of power, but *separate* from the master's institutions."[38] In much of his own work, however, Gutman goes too far in his attempt to shift the emphasis from slave "treatment", and comes dangerously close at times to writing the slaveholders out of the story completely.

Slave culture expressed itself in many ways, but two areas stand out in importance – religion and family life. Ironically, both have long been regarded as instruments of slave control in the hands of slaveholders. Certainly in the pre-Civil War decades slaveowners made considerable efforts, by use of white preachers, to inculcate spiritual and moral values which would lend safety and stability to the peculiar institution. It was of course an edited version of Christianity which was offered to the slaves, with a heavy emphasis upon the injunction that servants should obey their masters. Similarly, masters saw the family as an agent of discipline and order, as well as of population increase. But, whatever the vested interests of the masters, the slave community attached its own special importance to both institutions.

The richest and most perceptive account of slave religion is in Genovese's *Roll, Jordan, Roll.*[39] Christianity was a double-edged sword which could either sanction accommodation or justify resistance, but in the everyday routine of plantation life it brought spiritual comfort and relief to the individual slave, and sustaining power to the slave community. An emotional brand of Christianity, spiced with elements of the African religious legacy, developed into a distinctive Afro-American religion. Conjurors and magicians as well as Christian preachers wielded influence within the slave community. Emotional fervour and active participation – for example, in the characteristic call-and-response style – were features of slave prayer meetings which were often held away from the eyes and ears of the whites, and which were quite separate from the "official" religious services provided by the master. The emphasis of slave religion was on faith and love, not on rigid doctrine or formal structure; the most constantly re-iterated theme was deliverance and the coming of the promised land, in which the spiritual and the temporal were inextricably mixed. This was religion of joy and solace, not of shame or guilt.

Slave religion inspired a powerful sense of community and it threw up leaders and spokesmen for that community. But it did more. Levine has shown how it helped to provide alternative standards and alternative possibilities, especially in the area of relations between slaves, left largely untouched by the master's authority. The entire sacred world of the slaves, he says, "created the necessary space between the slaves and their owners and … the means of preventing legal slavery from becoming spiritual slavery. In addition to the world of the masters which slaves inhabited and accommodated to, as they had to, they created and maintained a world apart which they shared with each other and which remained their own domain, free of control of those who ruled the earth."[40]

The place where the slaves sought most of all to create "their own domain" was almost certainly within the family. Until recently the idea that the slave family was a bastion of the slaves' own life style would have seemed palpably absurd. The overwhelming power of the master, the lack of any legal status for slave marriage, the denial to the father of most of the normal parental role, the constant disruption of family life by slave sales, and the sexual exploitation of slave women by white men, were generally assumed to have wrecked the chances of survival of anything remotely recognizable as family life. A new and very different picture has now emerged. There was no legal marriage for slaves, but "marriages" were widely recognized and served important functions for the slave community as well as for the plantation. One-parent families existed in numbers and the maternal influence was everywhere strong, but the two-parent family predominated and slave fathers carved out a recognized role, despite all the difficulties. Sexual interference with slave women by white males was always a threat and often a fact, though not on the scale suggested by abolitionist propaganda. Such liaisons were sometimes voluntary, sometimes forced, usually casual but occasionally enduring; there were rare examples of slave mistresses who virtually assumed the role of the planter's wife. The double standards of a slave society were nowhere more apparent. Mrs. Chesnut, wife of a South Carolina planter, wrote mockingly that:

> Like the patriarchs of old, our men live all in one house with their wives and their concubines; and the mulattoes one sees in every family partly resemble the white children. Any lady is ready to tell you who is the father of all the mulatto children in everybody's household but her own. Those, she seems to think, drop from the clouds.[41]

Revealingly, she does not mention that slave families, too, had to live with the consequences of such liaisons.

The slave trade broke marriages and split families – and the threat of sale was a powerful weapon in the master's hand – but it did not break the institution of marriage and the family, or the belief in it. Fogel and Engerman have purported to show that the disruption was minimal, but their evidence and conclusions have failed to withstand close scrutiny. Perhaps as many as one quarter or one third of slave marriages were broken by such forced separation. Gutman's extensive researches have shown a curious pattern of stability and instability in marriage and family life. A stable "marriage" lasting many years could be broken by the sale of one partner at the master's whim, and the separated husband and wife were unlikely ever to meet again. After such forced separations, each would commonly take a new partner and perhaps start a new family – a pattern which Genovese labels "sequential polygamy".[42] Separation of parents and children was common especially as adolescent, single slaves were always among the most saleable. On the other hand, a sale occasionally united marriage partners belonging to different owners. Slaves were also sometimes sold in family groups, as the New Orleans auction notice displayed on the cover reveals. However, the notice also suggests that, if the nuclear two-parent family was the norm, there were many and varied deviations from it. (Of course, the "families" listed may not be complete.)

Because of the appalling strains and hazards which they faced, slave marriage and family life – and slave sexual mores – developed their own distinct character. Fogel and Engerman attempt to show the Victorian "prudishness" of slave sexual morality, but, to support their assertion, they rely almost entirely upon the claim that the average age at which women gave birth to their first child was surprisingly late. In a "non-contraceptive" society, this might well be significant, but their evidence is hotly disputed. Gutman argues plausibly that pre-marital sex was commonplace and incurred little disapproval, but that pregnancy or the birth of the first child normally marked a clear turning-point. The mother was expected to "marry" thereafter – though not necessarily to marry the father of the first child. One child by one father, and then a large family by a settled partner, was a common pattern. Pre-marital promiscuity was followed by marital respectability – although no set of sexual mores has ever guaranteed the latter. Slave marriage, says Gutman, was a licence for parenthood, not a licence for sex.

Lacking legal sanction, slave marriage developed its own wedding rituals from "jumping the broom" to formal religious services. Lacking wide choice, slaves found partners from neighbouring plantations, if not from their own community, and this often restricted married life to weekend conjugal visits. Lacking control over their own lives, slaves set their own standards and accepted the consequences of forced separation by tolerating "sequential" marriages. Lacking a sense of real security within the nuclear family, slaves established extended kin networks not merely in their own locality, but, spreading through sale and forced migration, far and wide across the South.

The slave family was the victim of adversity but also a positive response to it. Astonishment at its persistence under severe stress and enormous handicap may reflect an erroneous assumption that the institutions of marriage and family flourish fully only in a free society. Their long history in many different societies surely suggests otherwise. On the other hand, slave attitudes to sex and marriage also have a curiously modern ring – for example in the relaxed view of prenuptial sex, the pattern of "sequential polygamy", the normal presence of two working partners in a marriage, and the practical application of the principle of equality between the sexes.[43] The parallel is far from exact, of course; slave mothers, after all, commonly produced six, eight or ten children.

Gutman overstates his case that the slave family grew almost entirely from within the slave community. It existed after all on the sufferance of the slaveowner, and it was often shattered at his whim. Much of Gutman's own evidence – whether on the forced break-up of marriages, or the interference of masters with the domestic arrangements of their slaves – serves to emphasize this fundamental point. However, he is sometimes the victim of his own eagerness to demolish the arguments of other historians, and to demonstrate the autonomy and the "independence" of slave culture in general and the slave family in particular. For all that, the family was probably the most solid cement which the slave community had. It was also uniquely important in that the family linked generations of slaves and their cumulative experience. It was the most powerful transmitter of slave culture.[44] On this particular question, the historical insight of Herbert Gutman is at one with the imaginative insight of Alex Haley, whose novel *Roots* testifies to the strength of family feeling across the generations.[45]

The "culture" (in the more specialized use of the term) which the family helped to transmit has been brilliantly explored by Lawrence Levine in his recent book *Black Culture and Black Consciousness*. First, he offers a much-needed escape from the tangled issue of West African "survivals" in black American culture. There was no such thing as African culture, but the many diverse African cultures, Levine believes, had in common a certain style and emphasis. However, to search insistently for "survivals" of African culture is misleading, for aspects of old cultures, African and European, continued in the New World not as vestiges or relics but as dynamic contributions to a new group life. Resistance to change may suggest weakness in a culture; ability to respond, creativity and strength. The question is not one of survival but of interaction and transformation.

Music and dance, song and story offer rich evidence of the separate, independent life which slaves lived alongside their other existence of dependence upon their owners. They fostered a sense of community, and, in songs and the spirituals in particular, it was possible to voice criticism as well as to uphold cherished values. Slave music was a distinct cultural form, created and constantly re-created through a blending of individual and communal expression, as for example in the call-and-response pattern of many songs. The most persistent image of the spirituals is that of a chosen people on its way to the promised land. They are typical of slave religion in their sense of immediate personal contact with God; figures like Jesus and Moses were "significant others" in the life of many slaves. The sacred world of the slaves fused "the precedents of the past, the conditions of the present and the promise of the future into one connected reality." This sense of the oneness of things was reinforced by a firm belief, inherited from Africa, in a universe filled with spirits who could be invoked, or for that matter provoked. Magic, witchcraft and old folk beliefs lived side by side with slave Christianity. Belief in magic and luck were valuable supports in a way of life as unpredictable and uncontrollable as that of the slave.

Slave tales also helped to provide hope for the future and a survival kit for the present. Some were obviously tales with a moral, reinforcing religious beliefs, preaching the virtues of kindness, humility, family loyalty and obedience to parents, and sometimes submissiveness, or at least resignation, in the relationship with the master. However, even such moral tales also offered advice which was essentially practical, and this was much more true of the so-called "trickster" tales of the Brer Rabbit type. Such tales often had several layers of meaning and offered different lessons at different levels. Obviously they suggested how the weak might outwit, deceive or manipulate the strong. More broadly they outlined the tactics and attributes necessary to cope with an irrational world where good and right did not generally prevail. They may have been escape-valves for the pent-up frustration and bitterness of the slaves but they could also serve as cruel parodies of white society, exposing its pretension, hypocrisy and injustice to ridicule. The trickster figure could sometimes represent the master or some impersonal, irrational force, and not always the slave. There was an inevitable contradiction between the amoral strategy for survival recommended by the trickster tales and the standards and values taught by the moral tales or the spirituals. However, slaves learned to live with this contradiction because it reflected the tension in their daily lives. The two sets of "lessons" served different functions, and helped the slaves to live in the real world of the present while keeping alive their hope for the future. Religion, magic, folk beliefs, songs and spirituals, moral fables and trickster tales were all part of the distinctive cultural style of the slaves. Their supreme importance was to give the slave something which was unmistakably his own.[46]

One of the great problems of the recent historiography of slavery has been to reconcile a recognition of the severity and basic inhumanity of slavery with a conviction that the slave personality was not shattered by the experience and that slave culture not merely survived but prospered. Now perhaps it can be admitted that the total institution was not total, the closed society not completely closed, and the victims of the system not entirely helpless. They had enough strength to exploit their weakness and their dependence, and their masters had enough human weakness not to act fully upon the strength of the principle that slaves were merely property. Compromise, contradiction and compartmentalization filled the gap left between the extremes of total mastery and total surrender. Slavery inflicted terrible wounds and left permanent scars, but adversity can encourage as well as inhibit a powerful response. The response of slaves was powerful enough to keep alive the idea and the perception of freedom until freedom came.

6. Variations, exceptions and complications

A brief survey of the slave system must almost inevitably suggest a spurious uniformity, at odds with the untidy historical reality, and, like much longer works, give undue emphasis to the large plantation and to the Deep South. The balance may be redressed a little by a reminder of some of the variants and the exceptions – the edges of slavery – where its dividing lines, so often sharp and clear, become blurred and uncertain. Much of the character of an institution may be revealed by its margins and its abnormalities. Exceptions may not prove rules but they can put them into clearer perspective.

Urban and industrial slavery are two of the most obvious of those exceptions. The two are distinct from each other as most urban slaves were domestics, and most Southern industry was located in villages and small towns, or in the countryside. Never more than a small minority of the total slave population, urban slaves grew in numbers until the 1830s, but declined somewhat thereafter. In 1820 more than a fifth of urban dwellers in the South were slaves, in

1860 only a tenth. Slavery in the cities brought new problems of control for the whites and greater flexibility and discretion into the personal lives of the slaves. Many of the foundations of plantation discipline – isolation from outside influences, gang labour, and short and direct lines between master and slave – were eroded in the city environment. Industrial slavery tended to produce a similar loosening of the bonds. In the 1850s there were up to 200,000 slaves working in a variety of industries – textiles, processing of various agricultural products, mining, transport and construction – out of a total slave population nearing four million. Evidence suggests that slave-based industry could be at least as profitable as industry relying on wage labour, largely because slave labour was cheap. Firms with experience of both kinds of labour tended to prefer slaves. It is often said that slaves employed in industry endured some of the harshest treatment and the most ruthless exploitation which occurred anywhere in the South. On the other hand, there is evidence that, in the factory as on the plantation, there could be a complex and shifting balance between accommodation and resistance, conciliation and coercion, incentive and punishment, in the relationships between owner (or hirer) and slave.[47]

In both industry and the cities, the practice of hiring out slaves was more common than in agriculture. Such a slave might be contracted to work for a hirer for a period of a year, or he might be hired out day by day. Some slaves, often skilled craftsmen, were permitted to hire out their own services. They negotiated their own wages, and paid a fixed sum to their owners. These so-called "free slaves" operated close to the outer margins of slavery, and in a town with a floating population of hired slaves, runaways and free blacks, clear lines were very hard to draw.

The significance of these exceptional forms of Southern slavery can be interpreted in opposing ways. They may be seen as proof of the resilience, flexibility and adaptability of the peculiar institution – and, up to a point, this conclusion can hardly be denied. Slavery was predominantly agricultural, and slave labour was used mainly in the production of staples, especially cotton, but, so the argument would run, the system was not bound inseparably and permanently to cotton. It was simply that cotton was in enormous demand and yielded high profits. Claudia Goldin has explained the movement of slaves away from the cities in the 1840s and 1850s, not by their unsuitability for urban conditions, but by plantation demand for their labour. Free workers could replace slaves in the cities but not in the cotton fields.

The contrary view would be a social and racial rather than an economic one. Slave labour might be usable in factories and cities, but urban and industrial slavery, and hired slave labour, raised too many awkward questions about order and discipline and traditional sharp dividing lines not merely of status but of race and colour. Richard Wade suggests that urban slavery threatened to run out of control; what was tolerable and manageable in a numerically insignificant minority posed a serious threat if it were to become more than an exception to the rule. The Goldin thesis may explain the specific situation in the 1850s but not the wider and deeper problem.[48] The debate in the South on industrial slavery raised the question of priorities between race and class. Those who favoured industrial slavery argued that it would reinforce the slave system and maintain a clear line between the races; those who opposed it feared that it would eventually undermine slavery. Those who preferred to reserve Southern industry for white labour claimed that it offered economic opportunity to the poorer whites; the opposite view was that it would create an urban working class in the South and repeat the errors and the evils of Northern industrial society.[49]

The most conspicuous occupiers of the no man's land of Southern slave society were the free blacks. Most of them were the children of slaves freed during or just after the Revolution when the number of private manumissions was at its peak. In 1860 they numbered 260,000 or 6 per cent of the total black population, but the great majority were in the Upper South, 84,000 in Maryland alone. Maryland, indeed, had roughly equal numbers of free blacks and slaves. Many free blacks lived in an uneasy twilight world (although some prospered, and a few owned slaves themselves) and their presence was a constant embarrassment, and an anomaly, to the dominant white society. Their fluctuating fortunes made them a kind of barometer, measuring the condition of slavery itself.[50] Their safety, if any, lay in their small numbers. Again, as a small exception they could be tolerated, but right up to the coming of emancipation itself white American society, Northern as well as Southern, was nowhere near acceptance of the idea of a large, permanent population of free black citizens.[51]

The history of the Civil War years and of emancipation itself – the final "edge" of slavery – has also yielded many new insights, notably in the work of Genovese and Gutman, as well as in more specialized studies. The variety and ambivalence of the reactions of freed slaves to former masters, the eagerness of freed slaves to have their marriages legally confirmed, the strenuous efforts to reunite separated families, the extent to which mothers gave up work to care for children, the yearning for land as the foundation of the good life of a free citizen, all speak volumes about the character of slavery and the quality of slave life. After emancipation blacks received a larger share of the income generated by Southern agriculture, and they quickly seized the opportunity to make their own consumption decisions, and opted for more leisure and less work.[52] Such reactions cast a fresh light upon assertions about the rate of expropriation, belief in the Protestant work ethic, and the "negative nonpecuniary income" of slaves.

In the years of its pre-Civil War maturity, some of the internal contradictions of slavery intensified as the system became at once harsher and milder. The legal codes regulating slavery were stiffened, restrictions on free blacks tightened, the escape hatches were battened down more securely. On the other hand, the material conditions of slave life generally improved. Significantly, slaveholders showed a greater interest not only in the physical but the moral well-being of their human property. They were fascinated by the distinctive culture of the slave quarters, but anxious to impose upon it their own standards and values. They wished to absorb the blacks into the cultural mainstream of mid-nineteenth-century white America, but they were also determined to set them permanently apart. In the words of Joel Williamson, "the awful paradox of the last thirty years of slavery was that the black man was at the same time pulled into the white man's culture and kept stiffly at arm's length."[53]

If paradox is one of the underlying themes of Southern slavery, the other is the tension, ambiguity, and anxiety which resulted from the need to live with it – and which affected black and white alike Again an exceptional case – the murder of a white woman by her slaves, in South Carolina in 1861 – may serve to make the point. Mrs. Chesnut, a neighbour of the victim, confided her shocked and confused reactions to her diary:

> Hitherto I have never thought of being afraid of Negroes. I had never injured any of them, why should they want to hurt me? Two thirds of my religion consists in trying to be good to Negroes, because they are so in our power, and it would be easy to be the other thing. Somehow today I feel that the ground is cut away from under my feet.

Mrs. Chesnut's unease was more than matched by her sister who reported that her slave maidservant had insisted on sleeping in her bedroom to reassure her. "For the life of me," said her sister, "I cannot make up my mind. Does she mean to take care of me or to murder me?"[54] The double standards of a slave society created cruel dilemmas and agonizing doubts.

APPENDIX
The historiographical background

The historical debate over slavery began where the propaganda war between abolitionists and apologists for slavery had ended. Condemnation of slavery as a moral evil and a system of ruthless exploitation was pitted against respect for slavery as an effective system for the adjustment of relations between a superior and an inferior race. In the earlier decades of this century, the latter view predominated through the influence of U.B. Phillips and his school. His two main works, *American Negro Slavery* (1918) and *Life and Labour in the Old South* (1929),[2] (i.e. for full bibliographical details, see n.2) retain considerable interest although (or because) many of Phillips' preconceptions are now regarded as misconceptions.

The counter-attack against the Phillips school built up only gradually, but on several different fronts. Developments in economic history, sociology, social psychology and anthropology, and the works of a growing number of black historians brought new dimensions to the study of the subject.

After speaking in many voices during the 1930s and 1940s, the historical reassessment of slavery found its synthesis in Kenneth Stampp's *The Peculiar Institution* (1956).[3] Stampp's picture of a harsh but profitable institution became the new orthodoxy and it remains the most reliable and comprehensive account of slavery as a mature institution.

In the last twenty years, the old questions have not faded away but new ones have come to the fore. Historians have tackled them with a variety of new methods, and with a range of new assumptions and new priorities reflecting the racial crisis of modern America. If Stampp closed one chapter in the historiography of slavery, Stanley Elkins did more than anyone else to open another. His *Slavery* (1959)[5] set much of the agenda for subsequent debate, in its discussion of the comparative dimension of slave history and, above all, its probing of the slave personality. The controversy which Elkins stirred can be conveniently followed in Ann Lane, ed., *The Debate over Slavery* (1971).[33] Elkins replies to his critics in this volume and in the later editions of *Slavery* (1968, 1976). Stampp makes a thoughtful contribution to the debate in his article, "Rebels and Sambos: the Search for the Negro's Personality in Slavery", *Journal of Southern History*, **37** (1971), 367–93.

Discussion of the slave personality soon broadens out into related issues concerning the master–slave relationship, the quality of slave life and the evolution of slave culture. Among the briefer accounts of slave life are John Blassingame, *The Slave Community* (1972),[32] which is readable but uneven and too anxious to make an anti-Elkins point; Leslie H. Owens, *This Species of Property: Slave Life and Culture in the Old South* (New York: Oxford UP, 1976); and George P. Rawick, *From Sundown to Sunup: the Making of the Black Community* (Westport, Conn.: Greenwood, 1972), the somewhat fevered introduction to the multivolume set of slave narratives entitled *The American Slave: A Composite Autobiography*.

The most evocative and three-dimensional picture of slave life is in Eugene Genovese's *Roll Jordan Roll* (1974),[20] a sprawling, expansive book, stimulating to read but difficult to digest. It comes in the wake of his earlier, briefer, sometimes more polemical, always wide-ranging writings which reveal the incisive style and dialectical skill of a natural essayist. They include *The Political Economy of Slavery: Studies in the Economy and Society of the Slave South* (New York: Pantheon, 1967), *The World the Slaveholders Made: Two Essays in Interpretation* (New York: Pantheon, and London: Allen Lane 1969), and *In Red and Black* (1968–1972).[42] There is an interesting discussion of Genovese's work in R. H. King, "Marxism and the Slave South", *American Quarterly*, **29** (1977), 117–31.

Herbert Gutman, *The Black Family in Slavery and Freedom* (1976),[36] has placed the family squarely in the centre of slave life, and uses it as a tool to open up other aspects of slave culture. Gutman is inclined to assert more than his evidence demonstrates in a massive, somewhat repetitive and unnecessarily difficult book, which demands effort but also rewards it. The most exciting recent contribution to the study of slave culture is to be found in the earlier chapters of Lawrence Levine's *Black Culture and Black Consciousness* (1977),[1] which makes extraordinarily effective historical use of such evidence as slave songs, spirituals and folk-tales.

The comparative history of slavery has divided historians broadly into two camps: those who emphasize the cultural and institutional differences between slavery in various societies, and those who emphasize the common factors, arising mainly from the role of slavery as a system of economic exploitation. Among the former, Elkins draws heavily upon Frank Tannenbaum, *Slave and Citizen: the Negro in the Americas* (New York: Knopf, 1947). The latter group includes Eric Williams, *Capitalism and Slavery* (Chapel Hill: North Carolina UP, 1944), and, rather less certainly, David Brion Davis who, in two magisterial volumes, has added new dimensions to the subject: *The Problem of Slavery in Western Culture* (Ithaca: Cornell UP, 1966; London: Pelican, 1970) and *The Problem of Slavery in the Age of Revolution, 1770–1823* (Ithaca: Cornell UP, 1975). Carl N. Degler, *Neither Black Nor White: Slavery and Race Relations in Brazil and the United States* (New York: Macmillan, 1971), comes down even less certainly on the same side. There are two valuable collections of readings and essays: Laura Foner and Eugene Genovese, eds, *Slavery in the New World: a Reader in Comparative History* (Englewood Cliffs, N.J.: Prentice-Hall, 1969), and Engerman and Genovese, eds, *Race and Slavery in the Western Hemisphere* (1975).[25] See also the thoughtful article by Howard Temperley, "Capitalism, Slavery, and Ideology", *Past and Present*, **75** (1977), 94–118. Philip D. Curtin, *The Atlantic Slave Trade: a Census* (Madison: Wisconsin UP, 1969), has quickly acquired the status of a standard work. C. Duncan Rice, *The Rise and Fall of Black Slavery* (New York: Macmillan, 1975), is a spirited if somewhat uneven survey, and Nathan I. Huggins, *Black Odyssey: the Afro-American*

Ordeal in Slavery (New York: Pantheon, 1977), might be described as a superior, non-fictional equivalent of *Roots*.

Three outstanding studies of racial attitudes and racial problems in American history are Winthrop Jordan, *White over Black, 1550–1812* (1968),[6] George M. Fredrickson, *The Black Image in the White Mind: the Debate on Afro-American Character and Destiny, 1817–1914* (New York: Harper & Row, 1971), and C. Vann Woodward, *American Counterpoint: Slavery and Racism in the North–South Dialogue* (Boston: Little Brown, 1971).

The problem of slavery in revolutionary America is explored not only by Jordan and Davis, but also by Edmund S. Morgan, *American Slavery, American Freedom: the Ordeal of Colonial Virginia* (New York: Norton, 1975), Duncan J. Macleod, *Slavery, Race and the American Revolution* (Cambridge UP, 1974), and Robert McColley, *Slavery and Jeffersonian Virginia* (Urbana: Illinois UP, 1964; 2nd edn, 1973). See also J. R. Pole's review of Morgan and Davis, "Slavery and Revolution: the Conscience of the Rich", *The Historical Journal*, **20** (1977), 503–13.

If slave personality and slave culture have provided one of the main themes of recent historiography, the renewal and intensification of the debate on the economics of slavery has been the other. In his earlier books, listed above, Genovese emerged as the leading critic of the orthodox post-Stampp view, with its emphasis on slavery as a profitable business. He saw the slave South as a pre-capitalist society, in which slavery provided the foundation for a distinctive way of life and set of values but also condemned the South to economic backwardness. On the other hand, the case for the profitability of slavery was reinforced by a seminal article, based on econometric methods, by Alfred H. Conrad and John R. Meyer, "The Economics of Slavery in the Ante-Bellum South", *Journal of Political Economy*, **66** (1958), 95–130, and the same authors' *The Economics of Slavery and Other Studies in Economic History* (Chicago: Aldine Press, 1964).

Academic argument turned into popular sensation when the case for the efficiency and profitability of slavery was pressed further than ever before in Fogel and Engerman's *Time on the Cross* (1974).[4] The authors hoped to make their book a demonstration model of the new techniques of "cliometrics", but their claims were too often extravagant and their calculations too often highly questionable. The ensuing controversy has exposed the fallibility of "cliometrics". Because of their apparent exactitude, statistics can exercise a kind of tyranny over the unsuspecting, but the figures are often not exact at all. They are the end product of complex calculations based on information which is inevitably patchy and inadequate, and on a process of weighting one factor as against another which may not be much above the level of a hunch. The extent to which a small initial error can in consequence be magnified many times over in the final outcome, might itself be measured perhaps by a "geometric index of historical fallibility". Many of the most telling blows against *Time on the Cross* have been dealt by other quantitative historians. Some of the more important critiques have been collected in Paul A. David *et al.*, *Reckoning with Slavery* (1976).[14] There is no better overall discussion of *Time on the Cross*, in the context of other recent work on slavery, than Donald J. Ratcliffe, "The *Das Kapital* of American Negro Slavery? *Time on the Cross* after Two Years", *Durham University Journal*, **69**

(1976), 103–30, a highly perceptive and fair-minded evaluation which should be made more widely available. Roger Ransom and Richard Sutch, *One Kind of Freedom: the Economic Consequences of Emancipation* (1977),[17] sheds much light (most of it unflattering to *Time on the Cross*) on the economics of slavery itself, but seems likely to produce new clouds of controversy. Two useful readers, which predate *Time on the Cross*, are Harold D. Woodman, ed., *Slavery and the Southern Economy: Sources and Readings* (New York: Harcourt Brace, 1966), and Hugh G.J. Aitken, ed., *Did Slavery Pay? Readings in the Economics of Black Slavery in the United States* (Boston: Houghton Mifflin, 1971).

The "exceptions" to the Southern slave pattern have inspired a number of excellent monographs. On urban slavery, Richard Wade's *Slavery in the Cities* (1964)[49] should be used in conjunction with Claudia Goldin, *Urban Slavery in the American South* (1976).[26] Robert Starobin, *Industrial Slavery in the Old South* (1970),[28] and Ira Berlin, *Slaves without Masters* (1974),[50] both excel in using one specialized topic to shed light on the wider history of slavery.

The vigour of the historical controversy over slavery, and the proliferation of conflicting interpretations set problems for the relative newcomer to the subject. There is an outstandingly well-chosen cross-section of views in Allen Weinstein and Frank O. Gatell, eds, *American Negro Slavery: a Modern Reader* (New York: Oxford UP, 2nd edn, 1973; 3rd edn, 1978), which also has a very full bibliography. Our understanding of slavery has gained enormously from the cut and thrust of the historians' debate, but "adversary history" has its dangers, too. Real historical situations, and the real participants in them, may be obscured in the dust of the gladiatorial combat of the historians. This danger is enhanced by the propensity for historical model-building of a number of the protagonists. The intricate formulae and abstractions of *Time on the Cross* leave little room for real people, and Elkins' analysis of the slave personality makes but little allowance for the diverse personalities of individual slaves. Genovese struggles hard to force his enormous cast of characters into the mould of his intellectual and ideological formulation. Gutman, among others, criticizes Genovese for neglecting the processes of change over extended periods of time, but he in turn is reluctant to recognize the variations in the pattern of slave life between different parts of the South or between small farms and great plantations.

The best antidote to a surfeit of historiography is a return to the primary sources. A superb introduction to the sources is available in Willie Lee Rose's skillfully selected *Documentary History of Slavery in North America* (1976).[11] John W. Blassingame, ed., *Slave Testimony* (Baton Rouge: Louisiana State UP, 1977), is a fascinating but massive collection, and John White and Ralph Willett, eds, *Slavery in the American South* (London: Longmans, 1970), a useful brief selection, of source material.

From *Uncle Tom's Cabin* through *Gone with the Wind* to *Roots*, popular fiction has contributed more to myth-making than to historical understanding of slavery. But the myths are important, and the phenomenal success of Alex Haley's *Roots* (1976)[45] has its own meaning. If the reader always remembers that this is not history but fiction, he or she may overlook the needless historical errors and anachronisms, and appreciate some of the imaginative insights into what it was like to be a slave. However, some of the source material in Rose or in Blassingame is just as vivid and says at least as much.

APPENDIX
Bibliographical update

The 1970s witnessed a huge output of new work on the history of slavery in the Southern states of the United States. In particular, a number of landmark studies – notably by Eugene Genovese, Robert Fogel and Stanley Engerman, Herbert Gutman, Lawrence Levine and John Blassingame – contributed to a major reinterpretation and reassessment of almost every aspect of the subject. Since the late 1970s, there has been no one key book which offers a major reinterpretation of Southern slavery. However, there has been a steady flow of books which have either elaborated on the interpretive studies of the 1970s or sought to challenge or modify their conclusions. Much of this work has focused on particular aspects of the subject or on slavery in particular localities within the South, but there have also been some more general works, including attempts to survey and synthesize the more specialized studies published during the last two decades.

The cumulative effect of recent work has been to provide a more varied and sometimes more complex picture – more three-dimensional and more realistic than the bold generalizations of some of the major reinterpretations of the mid-1970s. These studies have been better able to convey something of the variations in slavery from place to place, changes over time in the character of slavery, and the complex web of human relationships which existed within and across the barriers imposed by a rigid system of bondage.

The list which follows is by no means comprehensive. It is a selection of some of the most important and influential recent books which is intended to suggest the continuing vitality – as well as the range and diversity – of slavery studies. No articles are included.

1. General Surveys and Introductions

John B. Boles, *Black Southerners, 1619–1869* (Lexington, KY, 1984)

Peter Kolchin, *American Slavery, 1619–1877* (New York, 1993; London, 1995)

Peter J. Parish, *Slavery: History and Historians* (New York and London, 1989)

2. Collections of Essays

George M. Fredrickson, *The Arrogance of Race: Historical Perspectives on Slavery, Racism and Social Inequality* (Middletown, CT, 1988)

Eugene Genovese and Elizabeth Fox-Genovese, *Fruits of Merchant Capital: Slavery and Bourgeois Property in the Rise and Expansion of Capitalism* (New York, 1983)

J. William Harris, ed., *Society and Culture in the Slave South* (London and New York, 1992)

Willie Lee Rose, *Slavery and Freedom*, edited by William W. Freehling (New York, 1982)

3. Slavery in the Colonial and Revolutionary Periods

Ira Berlin and Ronald Hoffman, eds, *Slavery and Freedom in the Age of the American Revolution* (Charlottesville, VA, 1983)

Allan Kulikoff, *Tobacco and Slaves: The Development of Southern Cultures in the Chesapeake, 1680–1800* (Chapel Hill, NC, 1986)

Mechal Sobel, *The World They Made Together: Black and White Values in Eighteenth-Century Virginia* (Princeton, NJ, 1987)

4. Economics of Slavery

Robert W. Fogel, *Without Consent or Contract: The Rise and Fall of American Slavery* (New York, 1989)

Gavin Wright, *The Political Economy of the Cotton South: Households, Markets and Wealth in the Nineteenth Century* (New York, 1978)

4a. Industrial Slavery

Fred Bateman and Thomas Weiss, *A Deplorable Scarcity: The Failure of Industrialization in the Slave Economy* (Chapel Hill, NC, 1981)

Charles B. Dew, *Bond of Iron: Master and Slave at Buffalo Forge* (New York, 1994)

Ronald L. Lewis, *Coal, Iron and Slaves: Industrial Slavery in Maryland and Virginia, 1715–1865* (Westport, CT, 1979)

5. Slave Life and the Slave Community

John W. Blassingame, *The Slave Community: Plantation Life in the Antebellum South*, revised and enlarged edition (New York, 1979)

John B. Boles, ed., *Masters and Slaves in the House of the Lord: Race and Religion in the American South, 1740–1870* (Lexington, KY, 1988)

Elizabeth Fox-Genovese, *Within the Plantation Household: Black and White Women of the Old South* (Chapel Hill, NC, 1988)

Ann Patton Malone, *Sweet Chariot: Slave Family and Household Structure in Nineteenth-Century Louisiana* (Chapel Hill, NC, 1992)

Albert J. Raboteau, *Slave Religion: "The Invisible Institution" in the Antebellum South* (New York, 1978)

Deborah Gray White, *Ar'n't I a Woman? Female Slaves in the Plantation South* (New York, 1985)

Betty Wood, *Women's Work, Men's Work: The Informal Slave Economies of Lowcountry Georgia* (Athens, GA, 1995)

6. Special Aspects

Drew Gilpin Faust, *James Henry Hammond and the Old South: A Design for Mastery* (Baton Rouge, LA, 1982)

Michael P. Johnson and James L. Roark, *Black Masters: A Free Family of Color in the Old South* (New York, 1984)

Michael Tadman, *Speculators and Slaves: Masters, Traders and Slaves in the Old South* (Madison, WI, 1989)

7. Local Studies

Orville Vernon Burton and Robert C. McMath, eds, *Class, Conflict and Consensus: Antebellum Southern Community Studies* (Westport, CT, 1982)

Randolph B. Campbell, *An Empire for Slavery: The Peculiar Institution in Texas, 1821–1865* (Baton Rouge, LA, 1989)

Barbara Jeanne Fields, *Slavey and Freedom on the Middle Ground: Maryland during the Nineteenth Century* (New Haven, CT, 1985)

J. William Harris, *Plain Folk and Gentry in a Slave Society: White Liberty and Black Slavery in Augusta's Hinterlands* (Middletown, CT, 1985)

Charles Joyner, *Down by the Riverside: A South Carolina Slave Community* (Urbana, IL, 1984)

8. Slavery and Southern White Society

William W. Freehling, *The Road to Disunion: Secessionists at Bay, 1776–1854* (New York, 1990)

Kenneth S. Greenberg, *Masters and Statesmen: The Political Culture of American Slavery* (Baltimore, 1985)

James Oakes, *The Ruling Race: The History of American Slaveholders* (New York, 1982)

James Oakes, *Slavery and Freedom: An Interpretation of the Old South* (New York, 1990)

Laurence Shore, *Southern Capitalists: The Ideological Leadership of an Elite, 1832–1885* (Chapel Hill, NC, 1986)

9. Comparative Studies

Shearer Davis Bowman, *Masters and Lords: Mid-19th-Century US Planters and Prussian Junkers* (New York, 1993)

George M. Fredrickson, *White Supremacy: A Comparative Study in American and South African History* (New York, 1981)

Peter Kolchin, *Unfree Labor: American Slavery and Russian Serfdom* (Cambridge, MA, 1987)

Roderick A. McDonald, *The Economy and Material Culture of Slaves: Goods and Chattels on the Sugar Plantations of Jamaica and Louisiana* (Baton Rouge, LA, 1993)

10. The End of Slavery

Ira Berlin *et al.*, *Slaves No More: Three Essays on Emancipation and the Civil War* (New York and Cambridge, 1992)

Leon F. Litwack, *Been in the Storm So Long: The Aftermath of Slavery* (New York, 1979)

Clarence L. Mohr, *On the Threshold of Freedom: Masters and Slaves in Civil War Georgia* (Athens, GA, 1986)

11. Reference Works

John B. Boles and Evelyn T. Nolen, eds, *Interpreting Southern History: Historiographical Essays in Honor of Sanford W. Higginbotham* (Baton Rouge, LA, 1987)

Randall M. Miller and John D. Smith, eds, *Dictionary of Afro-American Slavery* (New York, 1988)

NOTES

1. Lawrence W. Levine, *Black Culture and Black Consciousness: Afro-American Folk Thought From Slavery to Freedom* (New York: Oxford UP, 1977), p. 114.
2. Ulrich B. Phillips, *American Negro Slavery* (1918; reprinted Baton Rouge: Louisiana State UP, 1966), and *Life and Labor in the Old South* (1929; reprinted Boston: Little Brown, 1963).
3. Kenneth M. Stampp, *The Peculiar Institution: Slavery in the Ante-Bellum South* (New York: Knopf and Vintage, 1956).
4. Robert W. Fogel and Stanley L. Engerman, *Time On The Cross:* vol. 1, *The Economics of American Negro Slavery*, vol. 2, *Evidence and Methods* (Boston: Little Brown, 1974).
5. Stanley M. Elkins, *Slavery: A Problem in American Institutional and Intellectual Life* (Chicago UP, 1959; 3rd edn, 1976). For a fuller discussion of the historiographical background, see the Appendices.
6. Winthrop D. Jordan, *White Over Black: American Attitudes towards the Negro, 1550–1812* (Chapel Hill: North Carolina UP, 1968), pp. 80–2. Also available in abridged form under the title *The White Man's Burden* (New York: Oxford UP, 1974).
7. Gerald W. Mullin, *Flight and Rebellion: Slave Resistance in Eighteenth-Century Virginia* (New York: Oxford UP, 1972); James A. Henretta, *The Evolution of American Society,*

1700–1815: An Interdisciplinary Analysis (Lexington, Mass.: D. C. Heath, 1973), pp. 84–8.

8. The argument of this and the preceding paragraphs owes much to William W. Freehling, "The Founding Fathers and Slavery", *American Historical Review*, **77** (1972), 81–93.

9. Elkins, pp. 52–80.

10. Henretta, pp. 57–63.

11. Willie Lee Rose, ed., *A Documentary History of Slavery in North America* (New York: Oxford UP, 1976), p. 362.

12. Stampp, pp. 141–91.

13. Fogel and Engerman, 1, pp. 5–6, 148–57.

14. Gutman and Sutch, "Sambo Makes Good, or Were Slaves Imbued with the Protestant Work Ethic?" in Paul A. David, Herbert G. Gutman, Richard Sutch, Peter Temin and Gavin Wright (with an introduction by Kenneth M. Stampp), *Reckoning With Slavery: A Critical Study in the Quantitative History of American Negro Slavery* (New York: Oxford UP, 1976), pp. 55–93.

15. Fogel and Engerman, 1, p. 240.

16. Ibid., p. 205; *Reckoning With Slavery*, pp. 92–3; F. L. Olmsted, *A Journey in the Back Country* (1860; reprinted New York: Schocken, 1970), p. 82.

17. Fogel and Engerman, 1, pp. 153–7. David and Temin, "Slavery: The Progressive Institution?" in *Reckoning With Slavery*, pp. 186–9, 195–202; Richard Vedder, "The Slave Exploitation (Expropriation) Rate", *Explorations in Economic History*, **12** (1975), 453–7; Roger L. Ransom and Richard Sutch, *One Kind of Freedom: The Economic Consequences of Emancipation* (Cambridge UP, 1977), pp. 203–12.

18. Fogel and Engerman, 1, pp. 235–8.

19. Ibid., pp. 207–9.

20. Eugene D. Genovese, *Roll, Jordan, Roll: the World the Slaves Made* (New York: Pantheon, 1974), pp. 286, 292, and more generally pp. 285–324.

21. See, for example, Charles B. Dew, "Disciplining Slave Iron-workers in the Ante-Bellum South: Coercion, Conciliation

and Accommodation", *American Historical Review*, **79** (1974), 393–418.

22. The questions asked, and the distinctions made, in this and the following paragraphs owe much to Harold D. Woodman, "The Profitability of Slavery: A Historical Perennial", *Journal of Southern History*, **29** (1963), 303–25.
23. Fogel and Engerman, 1, pp. 192–6.
24. Wright, "Prosperity, Progress and American Slavery", in *Reckoning with Slavery*, pp. 302–33.
25. Fogel and Engerman, 1, pp. 44–58, 78–86; Gutman and Sutch, in *Reckoning With Slavery*, pp. 99–110, 154–61. Cf. Richard Sutch, "The Breeding of Slaves for Sale and the Westward Expansion of Slavery, 1850–1860", in Stanley L. Engerman and Eugene D. Genovese, eds, *Race and Slavery in the Western Hemisphere: Quantitative Studies* (Princeton, NJ: Princeton UP, 1975), pp. 173–210, and Engerman's comments, ibid., pp. 511–14 and 527–30.
26. Claudia D. Goldin, *Urban Slavery in the American South: A Quantitative History* (Chicago UP, 1976), pp.51–128.
27. Fogel and Engerman, 1, pp. 247–51.
28. *Reckoning With Slavery*, pp. 304, 349–52. Cf. Robert S. Starobin, *Industrial Slavery in the Old South* (New York: Oxford UP, 1970), pp. 186–9.
29. Lewis C. Gray, *History of Agriculture in the Southern United States to 1860*, 2 vols (Washington: Carnegie Institution, 1933–41) 2, p. 942.
30. Fogel and Engerman, 1, pp. 115–16; Sutch, "The Care and Feeding of Slaves", in *Reckoning With Slavery*, pp. 292–8.
31. Elkins, *Slavery*, pp. 81–139.
32. John W. Blassingame, *The Slave Community: Plantation Life in the Ante-Bellum South* (New York: Oxford UP, 1972), p. 201.
33. Ann J. Lane, ed., *The Debate over Slavery: Stanley Elkins and his Critics* (Urbana: Illinois UP, 1971), p. 350. See also the essays by Roy S. Bryce-Laporte, and by G. M. Fredrickson and C. Lasch, ibid., pp. 269–92 and 223–44.

34. Ibid., pp.225–8; Levine, *Black Culture and Black Consciousness*, pp. 54–5; Genovese, *Roll, Jordan, Roll*, pp.148–9.
35. Genovese, pp. 146–7.
36. Herbert G. Gutman, *The Black Family in Slavery and Freedom, 1750–1925* (New York: Pantheon, 1976; Oxford: Blackwell, 1976), p. 99.
37. Joel R. Williamson, "Black Self-Assertion before and after Emancipation", in Nathan I. Huggins, Martin Kilson and Daniel M. Fox, eds, *Key Issues in the Afro-American Experience*, 2 vols (New York: Harcourt Brace Jovanovich, 1971), 1, p. 219.
38. Gutman, p. 335.
39. Genovese, pp. 161–255.
40. Levine, p. 80.
41. Mary B. Chesnut, *Diary from Dixie*, ed. B. A. Williams (Boston: Houghton Mifflin, 1949), pp. 21–2.
42. Eugene D. Genovese, "American Slaves and their History", in *In Red and Black: Marxian Explorations in Southern and Afro-American History* (New York: Pantheon, 1968; Vintage, 1972), p. 112.
43. Ibid., pp. 112–13; Willie Lee Rose has made a similar point, for example in a lecture at the BAAS Conference at University College, Swansea, April 1978.
44. This whole discussion of the slave family relies heavily upon Gutman, *The Black Family*.
45. Alex Haley, *Roots* (Garden City, NY: Doubleday, 1976; London: Hutchinson, 1977, and Pan, 1978).
46. Levine, pp. 3–135 *passim;* quotation from p. 51.
47. Dew, "Disciplining Slave Ironworkers".
48. Richard C. Wade, *Slavery in the Cities: The South, 1820–1860* (New York: Oxford UP, 1964), pp. 243–81; Goldin, *Urban Slavery*, pp. 51–128.
49. Starobin, *Industrial Slavery*, pp. 191–214.
50. Ira Berlin, *Slaves Without Masters: The Free Negro In the Ante-Bellum South* (New York: Pantheon, 1974).
51. For the treatment of free Negroes in the North, see Leon

82

F. Litwack, *North of Slavery: The Negro in the Free States, 1790–1860* (Chicago UP, 1961).
52. Ransom and Sutch, *One Kind of Freedom*, pp. 2–6.
53. Williamson, "Black Self Assertion", p. 225.
54. Chesnut, *Diary from Dixie*, p. 140.